HOT & SPICY COOKING

Photography by Peter Barry
Recipes by Judith Ferguson, Lalita Ahmed and Carolyn Garner
Designed by Richard Hawke
Edited by Jillian Stewart

CLB 3261
© 1993 Colour Library Books Ltd, Godalming, Surrey, England
All rights reserved.
Colour separations by Advance Laser Graphic Arts, Hong Kong.
Printed and bound in Hong Kong.
ISBN 1 85833 028 9

HOT & SPICY COOKING

Colour Library Books

Contents

Introduction

Spices have been used in cookery for centuries. They are obtained from the aromatic parts of certain plants such as their pods, stems, seeds or roots. Considering their appearance, it is surprising just how precious spices were once considered to be. Many spices originated in the Far East, making them difficult to obtain and extremely costly for the first traders to import. Fortunately, today's methods of distribution mean we can all afford to enjoy their flavours and scents.

The popularity of spicy food has continued to grow, and although people still tend to associate spices with curries, there are a great many other dishes that use them to great advantage. This book features recipes from all over the world which include a variety of spices, some well known, others more unusual and exotic. In all the recipes the spices lend their own particular characteristics to the dishes, introducing new and exciting flavours to stimulate and transform your cooking.

Spices are sold either ground or whole, and are available in large or small quantities. It is best to buy most spices in small amounts as many of them will lose much of their flavour if stored over a long period of time. Obviously, the more you use a spice the bigger quantities you can buy it in. Black peppercorns, for example, can be bought in larger amounts as they are used regularly and are only ground immediately before use. If possible, it is best to grind your own spices rather than buy them ready-ground, as these are particularly susceptible to deterioration. Spices can be ground perfectly well with a pestle and mortar, but many people like to use a small coffee grinder that they keep just for this purpose. All spices should be kept in airtight jars and stored away from heat and light, or if they must be on show, they should be kept in storage jars with tinted glass.

As you might imagine, the range of hot and spicy foods is enormous, so we've gathered together a selection of recipes from around the world: Indian, Chinese, Spanish and Mexican cuisines are featured, together with recipes from the American Southwest and Bayou country.

Thanks to the pioneers of old, there is no need for you to travel to far-off places to experience spicy, exotic food. With the help of this collection, you can create delicious hot and spicy dishes in the comfort of your own home.

SPICY VEGETABLE FRITTERS WITH TOMATO SAUCE

This delicious dish makes an ideal starter or interesting snack.

SERVES 4-6

120g/4oz plain flour
120g/4oz wholemeal flour
1 tsp salt
1 tsp chilli powder
1 tsp ground cumin
280ml/½ pint water
1 tbsp lemon juice
1 small cauliflower, broken into small florets
1 aubergine, cut into 2.5cm/1 inch cubes
3 courgettes, trimmed and cut into
    2.5cm/1 inch pieces
225g/8oz button mushrooms
1 red pepper and 1 green pepper, seeded
    and cut into 5mm/¼ inch thick rounds
1 large potato, peeled and cut into
    2.5cm/1 inch cubes
400g/14oz tinned plum tomatoes, drained
1 red chilli, seeded and chopped
1 clove garlic, crushed
1 small onion, peeled and finely chopped
1 tbsp white wine vinegar
1 tbsp soft brown sugar
Salt and ground black pepper, to taste
1 sliced green chilli for garnish
1 sliced red chilli for garnish

1. Put the flours, salt, chilli powder and cumin into a large bowl. Make a slight well in the centre.

2. Gradually add the water and lemon juice to the flour, beating well until a smooth batter is formed.

3. Wash the fresh vegetables and allow them to drain completely on kitchen paper, or a clean cloth.

4. Put the tomatoes, fresh chilli, garlic, onion, vinegar and sugar into a food processor, or liquidiser and blend until the sauce is smooth.

5. Pour the sauce mixture into a small pan and heat gently, stirring until it is completely warmed through. Season with salt and transfer to a small serving dish and garnish with slices of red and green chillies.

6. Heat some vegetable oil in a deep fat fryer until it is warm enough to brown a 2.5cm/1 inch cube of bread in just under 1 minute.

7. Make sure the vegetables are completely dry, patting any moisture off them with kitchen paper if necessary.

8. Using a slotted spoon drop the vegetables, a few at a time, into the batter and dip them to coat thoroughly.

9. Remove the vegetables from the batter, again using the slotted spoon, and allow some of the batter to drain back into the bowl.

10. Drop the vegetables into the hot oil, and fry quickly until they are golden brown and the batter puffy.

11. Remove the fried vegetables from the oil and drain completely on kitchen paper, keeping them warm until all the remaining vegetables have been prepared this way.

12. Serve immediately, garnished with chilli peppers and serve the spicy tomato sauce alongside.

TIME: Preparation takes about 20 minutes and cooking takes about 30 minutes.

ANDALUCIAN AUBERGINES

*This delicious aubergine dish is highly reminiscent
of Andalucia in Spain where tomatoes, rice and
tuna fish are very popular ingredients.*

SERVES 4 as a snack or 8 as a starter

4 small aubergines
60ml/4 tbsps olive oil
1 small onion, finely chopped
1 clove garlic, crushed
120g/4oz cooked whole grain rice
200g/7oz can tuna in oil, drained and fish
   coarsely flaked
1 tbsp mayonnaise
1 tsp curry powder
4 fresh tomatoes, skinned, seeded and
   chopped
1 tbsp coarsely chopped parsley
Freshly ground black pepper

1. Cut the aubergines in half lengthways.
Score the cut surfaces lightly with a sharp
knife at regular intervals.

2. Brush the scored surface lightly with 1
tbsp of the olive oil and place the
aubergines on a greased baking sheet.

3. Bake the aubergines in a preheated
oven 190°C/375°F/Gas Mark 5, for 15
minutes, or until beginning to soften.

4. Cool the aubergines slightly, then
carefully scoop the centre flesh from each
half. Take care that you do not break the
skin at this stage.

5. Fry the chopped onion gently in the
remaining 30ml/2 tbsps of olive oil for 3
minutes, or until they are just transparent.

6. Add the garlic and the aubergine flesh,
and fry for a further 2 minutes. Season to
taste with pepper.

7. Add the rice, flaked tuna, mayonnaise,
curry powder, tomatoes, parsley and black
pepper to the aubergine mixture, and mix
together well.

8. Pile equal amounts of this rice and tuna
filling into the aubergine shells. Return the
filled aubergines to the oven proof baking
dish. Brush with the remaining olive oil,
and bake in the oven for a further 25
minutes. Serve piping hot.

TIME: Preparation takes 40 minutes and cooking takes about 50 minutes.

SERVING IDEA: Serve with a crisp mixed leaf salad and black olives.

VARIATION: For a tasty vegetarian variation, use 175g/6oz button mushrooms
in place of the tuna.

SPICED FRIED SOUP

Spicy and fragrant, this warming Indonesian soup is a meal in itself.

SERVES 4

4-8 tbsps oil
1 clove garlic, peeled but left whole
450g/1lb chicken breasts, skinned, boned
   and cut into small pieces
1 cake tofu, drained and cut into 2.5cm/
   1 inch cubes
60g/2oz raw cashew nuts
4 shallots, roughly chopped
1 carrot, very thinly sliced
90g/3oz mange tout
60g/2oz Chinese noodles, soaked for
   5 minutes in hot water and drained
   thoroughly
1.5 litres/2½ pints vegetable or
   chicken stock
Juice of 1 lime
¼ tsp turmeric
2 curry leaves
1 tsp grated fresh ginger
1 tbsp soy sauce
Salt and pepper

1. Heat some of the oil in a wok or large frying pan. Add the garlic and cook until brown. Remove the garlic from the pan and discard.

2. Add the chicken pieces to the wok and cook until they begin to brown. Remove the pieces and drain well.

3. Add a little more oil and fry the tofu until lightly brown. Remove and drain well.

4. Add the cashews and cook, stirring constantly until toasted. Remove and drain well.

5. Add a little more oil and fry the shallots and carrots until lightly browned. Stir in the mange tout and cook for 1 minute. Remove the vegetables from the pan and drain.

6. Heat the oil in the wok until it is very hot, adding more if neccessary. Add the noodles and cook quickly until brown on one side. Turn over and brown the other side.

7. Lower the heat and pour in the stock. Stir in the lime juice, turmeric, curry leaves, ginger, soy sauce and seasoning. Cover and simmer gently for 10 minutes, stirring occasionally, to prevent the noodles from sticking.

8. Add all the fried ingredients and heat through for 5 minutes. Serve immediately.

TIME: Preparation takes about 20 minutes and cooking takes about 20-25 minutes.

COOK'S TIP: If it is not possible to buy raw cashew nuts, use well rinsed and dried salted cashew nuts, and to not fry them in the oil.

PÂTÉ DE CAMPAGNE

This is the pâté of French restaurants known also as
pâté maison or terrine de chef. It should be coarse textured.

SERVES 10

340g/¾ lb pig liver, skinned and ducts
    removed
340g/¾ lb pork, coarsely minced
120g/4oz veal, coarsely minced
225g/8oz pork fat, coarsely minced
2 shallots, finely chopped
1 clove garlic, crushed
45ml/3 tbsps cognac
½ tsp ground allspice
Salt and freshly ground black pepper
1 tsp chopped fresh thyme or sage
225g/8oz streaky bacon, rind and bones
    removed
2 tbsps double cream
120g/4oz smoked tongue or ham, cut into
    6mm/¼ inch cubes
1 large bay leaf

1. Preheat the oven to 180°C/350°F/Gas Mark 4.

2. Place the liver in a food processor and process once or twice to chop roughly. Add the minced meats and fat, shallots, garlic, cognac, allspice, salt and pepper and thyme, and process once or twice to mix. Do not over-work the mixture; it should be coarse.

3. Stretch the strips of bacon with the back of a knife and line a terrine, metal baking pan or ovenproof glass dish. Stir the cream and the cubed tongue or ham into the meat mixture by hand and press into the dish on top of the bacon. Place the bay leaf on top and fold over any overlapping edges of bacon.

4. Cover the dish with a tight-fitting lid or two layers of foil and place the dish in a bain marie (dish of hand hot water) to come halfway up the sides of the terrine. Bake the pâté for 2 hours, or until the juices are clear. When it is done, remove it from the oven and remove the foil or lid.

5. Cover with fresh foil and weight down the pâté with cans of food or balance scale weights. Allow to cool at room temperature and then refrigerate the pâté, still weighted, until completely chilled and firm.

6. To serve, remove the weights and foil. Turn the pâté out and scrape off the fat. Slice through the bacon into thin slices.

TIME: Preparation takes 25 minutes, plus refrigerating until firm.
Cooking takes about 2 hours.

TAMARIND CHICKEN SATAY

*Traditionally satay is served as only a part of a meal,
but this version is so good that is needs only a
tomato sambal as an accompaniment.*

SERVES 4

---

4 chicken breasts, skinned, boned and
  cut into 1.25cm/½ inch cubes

Marinade
1 tbsp oil
5cm/2 inch piece tamarind, soaked in
  100ml/4 fl oz hot water or lemon juice
2 cloves garlic, crushed
1 tsp ground cardamom
½ tsp ground nutmeg
Salt and pepper
1 tsp kecap manis (sweet soy sauce)

Tomato and Chilli Sambal
2 red chilli peppers
1 small piece fresh ginger, grated
1 clove garlic, crushed
450g/1lb fresh tomatoes, peeled and
  seeded
4 tbsps oil
1 tbsps lemon or lime juice
1 tbsp dark brown sugar
Salt and pepper

---

1. Put the chicken in a large bowl. Mix
together the marinade ingredients and
pour them over the chicken. Stir well and
refrigerate for at least 30 minutes.

2. Grind together the chillies, ginger and
garlic in a food processor, or using a
pestle and mortar. Chop the tomatoes
coarsely and blend them into the chilli
mixture.

3. Heat the oil in a wok or large frying
pan and fry the tomato mixture for about
5-6 minutes, stirring occasionally to
prevent it sticking. Add the lemon juice
and a spoonful of water, if the sauce
becomes too thick.

4. Stir in the sugar and seasoning to taste.

5. Thread the marinated chicken cubes
onto thin wooden skewers.

6. Cook the chicken under a preheated
grill, turning frequently, until golden
brown – about 5-8 minutes. Brush the
chicken with the remaining marinade
during cooking. Serve with the tomato and
chilli sambal.

TIME: Preparation takes about 30 minutes, and cooking takes 10-15 minutes.

SERVING IDEA: Serve the satay on a bed of rice with the tomato and chilli sambal.

COOK'S TIP: If you cannot obtain tamarind use the juice of 2 lemons instead.
The kecap manis may be hard to find and can be replaced by ½ tsp dark
brown sugar and 1 tsp dark soy sauce.

SAMOSAS

*These crispy vegetable-stuffed triangles
can be eaten either hot or cold.*

SERVES 6

Pastry
275g/10oz plain flour
¼ tsp salt
¼ tsp baking powder
Water, to mix

Filling
3 tbsps oil
1 medium onion, chopped
450g/1lb potatoes, scrubbed and cut into
   small dice
2 carrots, grated
60g/2oz green peas, shelled
60g/2oz green beans, chopped
1 tsp chilli powder
1 tsp salt
1 tsp garam masala
½ tsp ground turmeric
1 tbsp lemon juice
Oil for deep frying

1. Make the pastry by sifting the flour, salt and baking powder into a bowl and adding enough water, a little at a time, to mix to a soft, pliable dough. Cover and leave to stand for 30 minutes.

2. Heat the 3 tbsps oil and fry the onion gently, until it is just soft. Stir in the potatoes and carrots and cook for 3-4 minutes.

3. Add the peas and beans to the potato mixture, cook for a further 2 minutes, then stir in the spices and lemon juice. Cover and simmer until the potatoes are tender. Remove from the heat and allow to cool.

4. Divide the dough into 12 equal-sized balls. Roll each piece out on a floured board, to a thin circle about 15cm/6 inches in diameter.

5. Cut each circle in half. Dampen the straight edges of each semicircle and bring them together, overlapping slightly to make a cone.

6. Fill each cone as it is made with a little of the filling, then dampen the open edge and seal by pressing together firmly. For extra firmness you may want to dampen and fold this edge over.

7. Heat the oil for frying. Fry the samosas, a few at a time, until they are golden brown on both sides. Drain on absorbent kitchen paper.

TIME: Preparation takes about 40 minutes and cooking takes about 25 minutes.

SERVING IDEA: Serve hot or cold with salad and an Indian chutney.

DAAL SOUP

Thick and hearty, this soup can be made
with either red or yellow lentils.

SERVES 6

350g/12oz red or yellow lentils
900ml/1½ pints water or stock
4 tinned tomatoes, drained and crushed
1 green chilli, sliced lengthways and
    seeded
2 tbsps natural yogurt or soured cream
15g/½ oz butter
1 medium onion, chopped, or sliced into
    rings
Salt and pepper
1-2 sprigs fresh coriander leaves, chopped

1. Wash the lentils in 4-5 changes of water. Drain them well and put them into a large pan with the water or stock.

2. Cover the pan and bring the lentils to the boil over a moderate heat. Reduce the heat and simmer for about 10-15 minutes, or until the lentils are soft. You may need to add extra water.

3. Using a balloon whisk, beat the lentils until they are smooth.

4. Add the tomatoes and chilli and simmer for 2 minutes, then stir in the yogurt or soured cream. Reheat, but do not boil.

5. Melt the butter in a small pan and fry the onion gently, until it is soft, but not coloured.

6. Discard the green chillies before eating the soup. Pour the soup into serving bowls and sprinkle over the chopped coriander leaves and the fried onions.

TIME: Preparation takes 15-20 minutes and cooking takes about 15 minutes.

SERVING IDEA: Serve with buttered brown bread or crisp rolls.

MEXICAN CHICKEN AND PEPPER SALAD

*This is the perfect lunch or light supper dish during the
summer, and it can be prepared in advance.*

SERVES 6

450g/1lb cooked chicken, cut into strips
140ml/¼ pint mayonnaise
140ml/¼ pint natural yogurt
1 tsp chilli powder
1 tsp paprika
Pinch cayenne pepper
½ tsp tomato purée
1 tsp onion purée
1 green pepper, seeded and finely sliced
1 red pepper, seeded and finely sliced
180g/6oz frozen sweetcorn, defrosted
180g/6oz long grain rice, cooked

1. Place the chicken strips in a large salad
bowl.

2. Mix the mayonnaise, yogurt, spices,
tomato and onion purées together and
leave to stand briefly for flavours to blend.
Fold dressing into the chicken.

3. Add the peppers and sweetcorn and
mix gently until all the ingredients are
coated with dressing.

4. Place the rice on a serving dish and pile
the salad into the centre. Serve
immediately.

TIME: Preparation takes about 30 minutes.

VARIATION: Add sliced or diced green chillies or Jalapeño peppers for a hotter flavour.
Try chilli sauce or taco sauce as an alternative seasoning.

SPICY FRIED FISH

The spice mixture is very hot, so use less if you want.

SERVES 4

4 fish fillets, about 225g/8oz each
225g/8oz unsalted butter
1 tbsp paprika
1 tsp garlic granules
1 tsp cayenne pepper
½ tsp ground white pepper
2 tsps salt
1 tsp dried thyme

1. Melt the butter and pour about half into each of four ramekin dishes and set aside.

2. Brush each fish fillet liberally with the remaining butter on both sides.

3. Mix together the spices and thyme and sprinkle generously on each side of the fillets, patting it on by hand.

4. Heat a large frying pan and add about 15ml/1 tbsp butter per fish fillet. When the butter is hot, add the fish, skin side down first.

5. Turn the fish over when the underside is very brown and repeat with the remaining side. Add more butter as necessary during cooking.

6. When the top side of the fish is very dark brown, repeat with the remaining fish fillets, keeping them warm while cooking the rest.

7. Serve the fish immediately with the dishes of butter for dipping.

TIME: Preparation takes about 20 minutes and cooking takes about 2 minutes per side for each fillet.

VARIATION: Use whatever varieties of fish fillets or steaks you like, but make sure they are approximately 2cm/¾ inch thick.

PRAWN CURRY

*A popular choice for lovers of spicy food, prawn curry
is simple to make and particularly tasty.*

SERVES 4

---

1 large onion, peeled and chopped
3 tbsps ghee or 3 tbsps salad or olive oil
1 inch cinnamon stick
6 green cardamoms
6 cloves
1 bay leaf
1 tsp ginger paste
1 tsp garlic paste
1 tsp chilli powder
1 tsp ground cumin
1 tsp ground coriander
½ tsp salt
1 green pepper, chopped into ½ inch
　　pieces
1½ cups tinned tomatoes, crushed
450g/1lb large prawns, peeled
2 green chillies, chopped
2 sprigs fresh green coriander leaves,
　　chopped

1. Fry onion in oil or ghee until just tender (3-4 minutes). Add cinnamon, cardamoms, cloves and bay leaf. Fry for 1 minute and then add ginger and garlic pastes.

2. Add chilli, cumin, coriander and salt. Fry for half a minute.

3. Add chopped green pepper and tomatoes, then bring to the boil.

4. Add prawns, cover and bring to the boil. Cook for 10-15 minutes.

5. Add chopped green coriander leaves and chopped chillies. Serve with plain boiled rice.

TIME: Preparation takes 15 minutes and cooking takes 20 minutes.

EGG CURRY

*Quick and easy, this curry is a delicious way
of serving hard-boiled eggs.*

SERVES 4

4-6 eggs
1 large onion
1 tbsp oil
2.5cm/1 inch stick cinnamon
1 bay leaf
4 small cardamoms
6 cloves
1 tsp garlic paste
1 tsp ginger paste
1 tsp ground coriander
1 tsp ground cumin
¼ tsp ground turmeric
1 tsp garam masala
1 tsp chilli powder
225g/8oz tinned tomatoes, crushed
Salt to taste
180ml/6fl oz water or vegetable stock
2 sprigs fresh coriander leaves
2 green chillies

1. Hard-boil the eggs in boiling water for 8-10 minutes. Cool them completely in cold water, then remove the shells.

2. Peel the onion and chop it finely. Heat the oil in a large saucepan and fry the onion gently for 2-3 minutes, until it is soft, but not browned.

3. Add the cinnamon, bay leaf, cardamoms and cloves and fry for 1 minute. Stir in the ginger and garlic pastes. Add the coriander, cumin, turmeric, garam masala and chilli powder. Stir together well and fry for 30 seconds.

4. Add the tinned tomatoes and salt to the spices. Stir in well and simmer for 5 minutes. Add the water or stock, and bring the mixture to the boil.

5. Put the eggs into the curry sauce and simmer for 10-12 minutes.

6. Chop the coriander leaves and the green chillies finely, and sprinkle them over the cooked eggs, to garnish.

TIME: Preparation takes about 10 minutes, and cooking takes 20 minutes.

SERVING IDEA: Serve with plain boiled rice.

MEE GORENG

These 'celebration stir-fry noodles' are of Indonesian origin and are so easy to prepare that they make an ideal quick lunch or supper dish.

SERVES 4

225g/8oz fine egg noodles
4 tbsps peanut oil
1 onion, finely chopped
2 cloves garlic, crushed
1 green chilli, seeded and finely sliced
1 tsp chilli paste
120g/4oz pork, finely sliced
2 sticks of celery, sliced
¼ small cabbage, finely shredded
1 tbsp light soy sauce
120g/4oz prawns or shrimp, shelled and
    deveined
Salt and pepper

1. Soak the noodles in hot water for 8 minutes, until they are soft. Rinse in cold water and drain thoroughly in a colander.

2. Heat the oil in a wok and stir-fry the onion, garlic and chilli, until the onion is soft and just golden brown.

3. Add the chilli paste and stir in well.

4. Add the pork, celery and cabbage to the fried onions, and stir-fry for about 3 minutes, or until the pork is cooked through. Season to taste.

5. Stir in the soy sauce, noodles and prawns, tossing the mixture together thoroughly and heating through before serving.

TIME: Preparation takes about 20 minutes, and cooking takes about 15 minutes.

VARIATION: Substitute sliced chicken breast for the pork.

SERVING IDEA: Serve with plain boiled rice and prawn crackers.

Shredded Beef with Vegetables

Stir-fried food is recognised as being extremely nutritious and wholesome.
This classic Chinese stir-fry is no exception, and has the bonus of
being extremely quick and easy to prepare and cook.

SERVES 4

225g/8oz lean beef steak, cut into thin
  strips
½ tsp salt
4 tbsps vegetable oil
1 red and 1 green chilli, cut in half, seeded
  and sliced into strips
1 tsp vinegar
1 stick celery, cut into thin 5cm/2 inch
  strips
2 carrots, cut into thin 5cm/2 inch strips
1 leek, white part only, sliced into thin
  5cm/2 inch strips
2 cloves garlic, finely chopped
1 tsp light soy sauce
1 tsp dark soy sauce
2 tsps Chinese wine, or dry sherry
1 tsp caster sugar
½ tsp freshly ground black pepper

1. Put the strips of beef into a large bowl and sprinkle with the salt. Rub the salt into the meat and allow to stand for 5 minutes.

2. Heat 1 tbsp of the oil in a large wok. When the oil begins to smoke, reduce the heat and stir in the beef and the chillies. Stir-fry for 4-5 minutes.

3. Add the remaining oil and continue stir-frying the beef, until it turns crispy.

4. Add the vinegar and stir until it evaporates, then add the celery, carrots, leek and garlic. Stir-fry for 2 minutes.

5. Mix together the soy sauces, wine or sherry, sugar and pepper. Pour this mixture over the beef and cook for 2 minutes. Serve immediately.

TIME: Preparation takes about 15 minutes, and cooking takes about 10 minutes.

SERVING IDEA: Serve with plain boiled rice and prawn crackers.

ALOO GAJJAR

*An authentic Indian potato dish which
is perfect as a snack or light lunch.*

SERVES 2-3

3 tbsps ghee or 2 tbsps salad or olive oil
1 tsp cumin seeds
2 medium potatoes, peeled and cut into
   ½ inch cubes
3 medium carrots, scraped and cubed
1 tsp chilli powder
1 tsp ground coriander
¼ tsp ground turmeric
Salt to taste
Juice of half a lemon

1. Heat ghee or oil and add cumin seeds.
When they begin to crackle, add potatoes.

2. Fry for 3-4 minutes then add carrots.
Stir the mixture and sprinkle with chilli,
coriander, turmeric and salt.

3. Stir fry the mixture for 1-2 minutes then
cover and cook on low heat for 8-10
minutes. Sprinkle with a little water to
help cook the carrots.

4. Sprinkle with lemon juice before
serving.

TIME: Preparation takes 10 minutes and cooking takes 10-15 minutes.

CHILLI WITH THREE BEANS

*Although called a soup, this dish is so hearty that
it is really a complete meal in itself.*

SERVES 6

3 tbsps vegetable oil
2 medium onions, roughly chopped
1 clove garlic, crushed
1 tbsp ground cumin
2 tsps paprika pepper
1 red or green chilli, seeded and chopped
675g/1½ lbs minced beef
790g/1¾ lbs tinned tomatoes
90g/3oz tomato purée
1 tsp oregano
1 bay leaf
140ml/¼ pint beer
Salt and pepper
120g/4oz each of tinned and drained
 red kidney beans, white kidney beans,
 pinto beans and chickpeas.

1. Heat the oil in a large pan. Add the onions and cook gently, until soft but not browned.

2. Add the garlic, cumin, paprika and chilli. Cook for 1 minute, before stirring in the beef.

3. Cook the meat until it is lightly browned, breaking it up with a fork, to prevent large lumps forming.

4. Stir in the tomatoes and their juice, the tomato purée, oregano, bay leaf and beer. Season to taste, then cover and simmer for 50 minutes, checking the level of liquid several times during cooking and adding a little water, if necessary.

5. Fifteen minutes before the end of the cooking time, stir in the drained beans and chickpeas.

TIME: Preparation takes 30 minutes, and cooking takes about 1 hour.

SERVING IDEA: Serve the soup with corn or tortilla chips and a garnish of
 sour cream, grated cheese, diced avocado, or chopped spring onions.

AUBERGINES AND PEPPERS SZECHUAN STYLE

Authentic Szechuan food is fiery hot. Outside China,
restaurants often tone down the taste for Western palates.

SERVES 2-3

1 large aubergine
2 cloves garlic, crushed
2.5cm/1 inch piece fresh ginger, shredded
1 onion, cut into 2.5cm/1 inch pieces
1 small green pepper, seeded, cored and
  cut into 2.5cm/1 inch pieces
1 small red pepper, seeded, cored and cut
  into thin strips
1 red or green chilli, seeded, cored and
  cut into thin strips
120ml/4 fl oz chicken or vegetable stock
5ml/1 tsp sugar
5ml/1 tsp vinegar
Pinch salt and pepper
5ml/1 tsp cornflour
15ml/1 tbsp soy sauce
Dash sesame oil
Oil for cooking

1. Cut the aubergine in half and score the surface.

2. Sprinkle lightly with salt and leave to drain in a colander or on paper towels for 30 minutes.

3. After 30 minutes, squeeze the aubergine gently to extract any bitter juices and rinse thoroughly under cold water. Pat dry and cut the aubergine into 2.5cm/1 inch cubes.

4. Heat about 45ml/3 tbsps oil in a wok. Add the aubergine and stir-fry for about 4-5 minutes. It may be necessary to add more oil as the aubergine cooks. Remove from the wok and set aside.

5. Reheat the wok and add 30ml/2 tbsps oil. Add the garlic and ginger and stir-fry for 1 minute. Add the onions and stir-fry for 2 minutes. Add the green pepper, red pepper and chilli pepper and stir-fry for 1 minute. Return the aubergine to the wok along with the remaining ingredients.

6. Bring to the boil, stirring constantly, and cook until the sauce thickens and clears. Serve immediately.

TIME: Preparation takes about 30 minutes and cooking takes about 7-8 minutes.

SERVING IDEA: Serve as a vegetarian stir-fry dish with plain or fried rice, or serve as a side dish.

PENNE WITH SPICY CHILLI SAUCE

Penne are hollow pasta tubes which can be bought at most supermarkets.
Macaroni can be used equally as well.

SERVES 4-6

450g/1lb tinned plum tomatoes
1 tbsp olive oil
2 cloves garlic, crushed
1 onion, chopped
4 rashers of bacon, chopped
2 red chilli peppers, seeded and chopped
2 spring onions, chopped
60g/2oz Pecorino or Parmesan cheese,
    grated
450g/1lb penne or macaroni
Salt and pepper

1. Chop the tomatoes and sieve them to remove the pips.

2. Heat the oil in a frying pan and fry the garlic, onion and bacon gently for 6-8 minutes.

3. Add the sieved tomatoes, the chilli peppers, chopped spring onions and half of the cheese. Simmer gently for 20 minutes.

4. Cook the penne or macaroni in boiling water for 10-15 minutes, or until tender. Rinse under hot water and drain well.

5. Put the cooked penne into a warm serving dish and toss them in half of the sauce. Pour the remaining sauce over the top and sprinkle with the remaining cheese.

TIME: Preparation takes about 15 minutes, and cooking takes about 40 minutes.

VARIATION: Substitute 60g/2oz chopped button mushrooms for the bacon.

SERVING IDEA: Garnish the serving dish with spring onion flowers and serve with a mixed green salad.

VINDALOO

A vindaloo is one of the hottest curries and not for the faint-hearted!
Beef or lamb can also be cooked in the same way.

SERVES 4-6

1 tbsp oil
3 cloves garlic, crushed
¼ tsp each of ground cumin, coriander,
   cinnamon, cloves, black pepper, ginger
1½ tsps turmeric
1 tsp mustard seed
450g/1lb pork fillet, cut into cubes
3 bay leaves
4 tbsps tamarind extract
2 tsps tomato purée
2 tsps sugar
3 tbsps vinegar
Water or stock to moisten
1-2 green chillies, seeded and chopped
Salt
1 tbsp cornflour mixed with 3 tbsps water
   or stock (optional)

1. Melt the oil in a frying pan and add the garlic, spices, and mustard seed. Cook for 3-4 minutes.

2. Allow to cool and pour over the pork cubes in a shallow dish. Stir to coat and add the bay leaves. Leave to marinate overnight in the refrigerator, stirring occasionally.

3. Mix the tamarind, tomato purée, sugar and vinegar and pour over the meat.

4. Add water or stock to come a quarter of the way up the meat, and sprinkle over the chillies. Cover the dish and cook in a preheated oven at 180°C/325°F/Gas Mark 4 for about 40 minutes, adding more water or stock if the mixture begins to dry out.

5. If desired, the sauce may be thickened with the cornflour and water or stock. Cook for 2-3 minutes or until clear.

TIME: Preparation takes about 20 minutes, but meat should marinate overnight for full flavour. Cooking takes about 40 minutes.

SPICED CHICKPEAS

*This very fragrant curry is delicious either on its
own, or as part of a larger Indian meal.*

SERVES 6

450g/1lb chickpeas, soaked overnight in
   cold water
3 tbsps oil
1 large onion, chopped
2 bay leaves
2 green chillies, sliced in half lengthways
2.5cm/1 inch piece cinnamon stick
2.5cm/1 inch piece fresh root ginger,
   grated
4 cloves garlic, crushed
1½ tsps ground coriander
4 cloves, ground
1 tsp cumin seeds, ground
Seeds of 4 large black cardamoms, ground
Seeds of 4 small cardamoms, ground
300ml/10fl oz tinned tomatoes, chopped
½ tsp black pepper
½ tsp salt
6 sprigs fresh coriander leaves, chopped

1. Cook the chickpeas in their soaking water, until they are soft. Drain and reserve 225ml/8fl oz of the cooking liquid.

2. Heat the oil in a frying pan and fry the onion gently, until soft, but not coloured. Add the bay leaves, chillies, cinnamon, ginger and garlic and fry for a further minute.

3. Stir in the ground spices, the tomatoes and the salt and pepper.

4. Add the reserved chickpea cooking liquid and the drained chickpeas. Mix well. Sprinkle with the chopped coriander leaves, cover and simmer for 10 minutes, adding a little extra liquid, if necessary.

TIME: Preparation takes about 15 minutes, plus overnight soaking and
cooking takes about 45-50 minutes.

RED BEAN CURRY

This colourful curry is very easy to make.
The beans must be cooked thoroughly before use.

SERVES 4

225g/8oz dried red kidney beans,
   soaked overnight
3 tbsps oil
2 medium onions, chopped
1 bay leaf
2.5cm/1 inch piece cinnamon stick
6 cloves
Seeds of 6 green cardamoms
2 green chillies, quartered
3 cloves garlic, crushed
2.5cm/1 inch piece fresh root ginger,
   grated
½ tsp chilli powder
¼ tsp ground turmeric
1½ tsps ground coriander
1 tsp ground cumin
1 tsp garam masala
425g/15oz canned tomatoes, chopped
½ tsp salt
2-3 sprigs fresh coriander leaves, chopped

---

1. Cook the kidney beans, boiling them rapidly for 10 minutes and then simmering for at least 30 minutes, until they are soft. Remove from the heat and allow them to cool in the cooking liquid.

2. Heat the oil in a large saucepan and cook the onions, until they are soft. Add the bay leaf, cinnamon, cloves and cardamoms and fry for 1 minute.

3. Add the green chillies, garlic and ginger, and fry for about 30 seconds, before mixing in the ground spices and cooking for a further 30 seconds, stirring continuously, to prevent them burning.

4. Add the tomatoes and season with salt.

5. Drain the beans and reserve the cooking liquid. Add the beans to the tomatoes and mix well, bring to the boil, then stir in 280ml/½ pint of the bean liquid.

6. Simmer for 10 minutes, then stir in the chopped coriander.

TIME: Preparation takes about 15 minutes, plus overnight soaking and cooking takes about 45 minutes.

VARIATION: Use any of the different types of dried beans, instead of the red kidney beans.

CARIBBEAN PRAWN AND SWEET POTATOES IN COCONUT SAUCE

Sweet potatoes are now widely available in most supermarkets and this recipe makes delicious use of them.

SERVES 6

450g/1lb sweet potatoes, peeled and diced
1 large onion, chopped
1 clove garlic, crushed
2.5cm/1 inch piece of fresh ginger, grated
1 red or green chilli pepper, seeded
   and chopped
¼ tsp ground cumin
¼ tsp ground coriander
¼ tsp ground allspice
2 tbsps coconut cream, or 15g/½ oz
   creamed coconut, dissolved in
   2 tbsps boiling water
570ml/1 pint water
120g/4oz peeled prawns
120g/4oz chicory, shredded
225/8oz Chinese leaves, shredded
1 tbsp dark brown sugar
2 tbsps lime juice
Salt
Desiccated coconut, to sprinkle

1. In a large saucepan, mix together the sweet potatoes, onion, garlic, ginger, chilli pepper, spices, coconut cream and water.

2. Bring to the boil and simmer until the potato is almost tender.

3. Add the prawns, chicory and Chinese leaves. Simmer for 4-5 minutes, until the ingredients are warmed through, but the leaves are still crisp.

4. Add the sugar and lime juice and season to taste.

5. Serve sprinkled with the desiccated coconut.

TIME: Preparation takes about 20 minutes and cooking takes 20-30 minutes.

SERVING IDEA: Serve with boiled rice, mixed with cooked peas and sweetcorn.

VARIATION: Yams are a white version of sweet potato and can be used in this recipe equally as well.

CHILLI PRAWN QUICHE

Fresh chilli peppers give a Mexican flavour
to this quiche with its prawn filling.

SERVES 6

Pastry
120g/4oz plain flour
Pinch salt
30g/2 tbsps butter or margarine
30g/2 tbsps white cooking fat
30-60ml/2-4 tbsps cold water

Filling
4 eggs
140ml/¼ pint milk
140ml/¼ pint single cream
¼ clove garlic, crushed
120g/4oz Cheddar cheese, grated
3 spring onions, chopped
2 green chillies, seeded and chopped
225g/8oz cooked and peeled prawns
Salt
Cooked, unpeeled prawns and parsley
   for garnish

1. Sift the flour with a pinch of salt into a mixing bowl, or place in a food processor and mix once or twice.

2. Rub in the butter and fat until the mixture resembles fine breadcrumbs, or work in the food processor, being careful not to over-mix.

3. Mix in the liquid gradually, adding enough to bring the pastry together in a ball. In a food processor, add the liquid through the funnel while the machine is running.

4. Wrap the pastry well and chill for 20-30 minutes.

5. Roll out the pastry on a well-floured surface with a floured rolling pin.

6. Wrap the circle of pastry around the rolling pin to lift it into a 25cm/10 inch flan dish. Unroll the pastry over the dish.

7. Carefully press the pastry onto the bottom and up the sides of the dish, taking care not to stretch it.

8. Roll the rolling pin over the top of the dish to remove excess pastry, or cut off with a sharp knife.

9. Mix the eggs, milk, cream and garlic together. Sprinkle the cheese, onion, chillies and prawns onto the base of the pastry and pour over the egg mixture.

10. Bake in a preheated 200°C/400°F/Gas Mark 6 oven for 30-40 minutes until firm and golden brown. Peel the tail shells off the prawns and remove the legs and roe if present. Use to garnish the quiche along with the sprigs of parsley.

TIME: Preparation takes about 40 minutes, which includes time for the pastry to chill.
Cooking takes 30-40 minutes.

PORK WITH LIME AND CHILLI

Creamy coconut and fragrant spices blend together
to complement the pork beautifully.

SERVES 4

1 clove garlic, crushed
1 tsp brown sugar
1 tsp oil
1 tsp lime juice
1 tsp cornflour
450g/1lb lean pork, cut into 2.5cm/1 inch
  cubes
140ml/¼ pint oil, for deep-frying
1 green chilli, seeded and thinly sliced
1 red chilli, seeded and thinly sliced
8 spring onions, trimmed and sliced
  diagonally
1 tsp ground turmeric
1 tsp ground coriander
1 tsp ground cumin
1 tsp ground nutmeg
Pinch ground cloves
4 tbsps soy sauce
Juice and rind of 1 lime
140ml/¼ pint coconut milk
Salt and pepper

1. Combine the garlic, sugar, oil, lime juice and cornflour in a large bowl. Stir in the pork and coat thoroughly with the garlic and lime juice mixture. Allow to stand in the refrigerator for at least 1 hour.

2. Heat the oil for frying in a wok and add the pork cubes. Cook, stirring frequently, for about 10 minutes until golden brown and cooked through. Drain and set aside.

3. Remove all except about 1 tbsp of the oil. Reheat and add the chillies and onions. Stir-fry for about 2 minutes.

4. Add the ground spices and fry for a further 30 seconds. Stir in the remaining ingredients and bring to the boil.

5. Add the fried pork to the sauce and heat through. Adjust the seasoning and serve.

TIME: Preparation takes about 20 minutes, plus at least 1 hour marinating.
Cooking takes about 20 minutes.

CHICKEN TIKKA

Red food colouring gives this dish its traditional appearance,
but the taste will not be affected if you prefer not to use it.

SERVES 4-6

140ml/¼ pint natural yogurt
1 tsp chilli powder
2 tsps ginger paste
2 tsps garlic paste
2 tsps garam masala
½ tsp salt
¼ tsp red food colouring
Juice of 1 lemon
1.5kg/3lb roasting chicken, cut into
   8-10 pieces
Oil for brushing

1. In a large bowl, mix together the yogurt, chilli powder, ginger and garlic pastes, garam masala, salt, colouring and lemon juice.

2. Add the chicken pieces to the yogurt mixture and mix in well to ensure they are evenly coated.

3. Line a grill pan with aluminium foil and arrange the chicken pieces on this, together with the yogurt sauce. Preheat the grill to moderate and grill the chicken pieces for about 5-6 minutes on each side, brushing with a little oil if necessary, to prevent them burning.

TIME: Preparation takes about 10 minutes, and cooking takes about 30 minutes.

SERVING IDEA: Serve with wedges of lemon and a crisp lettuce and tomato salad.

SPICED BEEF

*Fragrant and spicy, this delicious Chinese
dish is quick and easy to make.*

SERVES 4

450g/1lb fillet of beef
1 tsp soft brown sugar
2-3 star anise, ground
½ tsp ground fennel
1 tbsp dark soy sauce
2.5cm/1 inch piece fresh root ginger,
 grated
½ tsp salt
2 tbsps vegetable oil
6 spring onions, sliced
1 tbsp light soy sauce
½ tsp freshly ground black pepper

1. Cut the beef into thin strips 2.5cm/1 inch long.

2. In a bowl, mix together the sugar, spices and dark soy sauce.

3. Put the beef, ginger and salt into the soy sauce mixture and stir well to coat evenly. Cover and allow to stand for 20 minutes.

4. Heat the oil in a work or large frying pan and stir-fry the onions quickly for 1 minute.

5. Add the beef and fry, stirring constantly, for 4 minutes, or until the meat is well browned.

6. Stir in the soy sauce and black pepper and cook gently for a further 1 minute.

TIME: Preparation takes about 30 minutes, and cooking takes 5-6 minutes.

SERVING IDEA: Serve the beef with a spicy dip.

CHICKEN TOMATO

Made with a very fragrant selection of spices,
this dish is sure to become a firm favourite.

SERVES 4-6

1 onion, peeled and chopped
3 tbsps oil
2.5cm/1 inch piece cinnamon stick
1 bay leaf
6 cloves
Seeds of 6 small cardamoms
2.5cm/1 inch piece fresh ginger, grated
4 cloves garlic, crushed
1.5kg/3lb roasting chicken, cut into
   8-10 pieces
1 tsp chilli powder
1 tsp ground cumin
1 tsp ground coriander
400g/14oz tinned tomatoes, chopped
1 tsp salt
2 sprigs fresh coriander leaves, chopped
2 green chillies, halved and seeded

1. In a large saucepan, fry the onion in the oil, until it has softened. Add the cinnamon, bay leaf, cloves, cardamom seeds, ginger and garlic. Fry for 1 minute.

2. Add the chicken pieces to the saucepan. Sprinkle the chilli powder, ground cumin and coriander over the chicken in the pan. Fry for a further 2 minutes, stirring continuously, to ensure the spices do not burn.

3. Stir in the remaining ingredients, mixing well to blend the spices evenly. Cover the pan and simmer for 40-45 minutes, or until the chicken is tender.

TIME: Preparation takes about 30 minutes and cooking takes about 40-50 minutes.

CHICKEN MOGHLAI WITH CORIANDER CHUTNEY

The creamy spiciness of the chicken is a good contrast to the hotness of the chutney.

SERVES 4-6

4 tbsps oil
1.5kg/3lbs chicken pieces, skinned
1 tsp ground cardamom
½ tsp ground cinnamon
1 bay leaf
4 cloves
2 onions, finely chopped
2.5cm/1 inch piece fresh ginger, grated
4 cloves garlic, crushed
30g/1oz ground almonds
2 tsps cumin seeds
Pinch cayenne pepper
280ml/½ pint single cream
6 tbsps natural yogurt
2 tbsps roasted cashew nuts
2 tbsps sultanas
Salt

Chutney
90g/3oz coriander leaves
1 green chilli pepper, chopped and seeded
1 tbsp lemon juice
Salt and pepper
Pinch sugar
1 tbsp oil
½ tsp ground coriander

1. To prepare the chicken, heat the oil in a large frying pan. Fry the chicken pieces on each side until golden brown.

2. Remove the chicken and set aside. Put the cardamom, cinnamon, bay leaf and cloves into the hot oil and meat juice and fry for 30 seconds. Stir in the onions and fry until soft, but not brown.

3. Stir the ginger, garlic, almonds, cumin and cayenne pepper into the onions. Cook gently for 2-3 minutes, then stir in the cream.

4. Return the chicken pieces to the pan, along with any juices. Cover and simmer gently for 30-40 minutes, or until the chicken is cooked and tender.

5. Whilst the chicken is cooking, prepare the chutney. Put the coriander leaves, chilli, lemon, seasoning and sugar into a blender or food processor and work to paste.

6. Heat the oil and cook the ground coriander for 1 minute. Add this mixture to the processed coriander leaves and blend in thoroughly.

7. Just before serving, stir the yogurt, cashews and sultanas into the chicken. Heat through just enough to plump up the sultanas, but do not allow the mixture to boil.

8. Serve at once with the chutney.

TIME: Preparation takes about 25 minutes, and cooking takes 30-40 minutes.

SERVING IDEA: Serve with boiled rice and a cucumber and tomato salad.

AUBERGINE BAKE

*This substantial aubergine main course has an unusual
flavour which is sure to keep your family, or friends,
guessing about the mixture of ingredients.*

SERVES 6

3 large aubergines
2 tsps freshly ground sea salt
Malt vinegar
2 tbsps sunflower oil
2 large onions, sliced
2 fresh green chillies, seeded and chopped
425g/15oz can peeled tomatoes, chopped
½ tsp chilli powder
1 tsp crushed garlic
½ tsp ground turmeric
Vegetable oil, for deep-frying
4 tbsps natural yogurt, or 1% fat
   fromage frais
1 tsp freshly ground black pepper
4 tomatoes, thinly sliced
180g/6oz Edam cheese, finely grated

1. Cut the aubergines into 5mm/¼ inch thick slices. Lay the slices in a shallow dish, and sprinkle with 1 tsp of the salt and enough malt vinegar to cover.

2. Allow the aubergine to marinate for 20-30 minutes. Drain thoroughly.

3. Heat the sunflower oil in a frying pan, and fry the onions gently, until they are golden brown. Add the chillies, chopped tomatoes, chilli powder, garlic, turmeric and the remaining salt. Mix well, and simmer for 5-7 minutes.

4. Remove the pan from the heat and leave the tomato mixture to cool.

5. Put the tomato mixture into a food processor, or liquidizer, and blend until smooth. Set aside.

6. Heat the vegetable oil for deep-frying, and deep-fry the drained, marinaded aubergine, until they are golden brown, approximately 2-3 minutes.

7. Drain the fried aubergine slices on absorbent kitchen paper.

8. Grease a large, deep baking dish and arrange half the fried aubergine slices, closely together, in the bottom of the dish.

9. Cover the aubergine slices in the dish with half the tomato sauce and half the yogurt, or fromage frais. Sprinkle with the black pepper.

10. Place the remaining aubergine slices over the yogurt and top with the remaining sauce and the remaining yogurt.

11. Arrange the tomato slices on top and sprinkle with the grated cheese. Bake in a preheated oven, 180°C/35°F/Gas Mark 4, for 10-15 minutes, or until the cheese has melted and turned golden brown.

TIME: Preparation takes about 30 minutes and cooking takes about 30-40 minutes.

SERVING IDEA: Serve hot, as a main course, with wholemeal bread, or pitta bread.

PIQUANT PORK CHOPS

*The spicy sauce in this recipe completely
transforms the humble pork chop.*

SERVES 4

4 lean pork chops, trimmed of fat and rind
1 tbsp polyunsaturated vegetable oil
1 small onion, chopped
1 tbsp unrefined brown sugar
1 tbsp dry mustard, any flavour
2 tsps tomato purée
1 beef stock cube
280ml/½ pint water
1 tbsp Worcestershire sauce
2 tbsps fresh lemon juice

1. Grill the pork chops under a preheated hot grill for 6-7 minutes on each side.

2. Heat the oil in a large frying pan, and fry the onion gently, until it is lightly browned.

3. Stir the sugar, mustard powder, tomato purée and beef stock cube into the cooked onion. Mix the ingredients together well, then add the water and bring to the boil, stirring continuously.

4. Stir the Worcestershire sauce and the lemon juice into the onion and spice mixture, then check the seasoning, adding freshly ground sea salt and black pepper to taste.

5. Put the pork chops into an ovenproof baking dish, or shallow casserole, and pour the sauce over them.

6. Cook in a preheated oven, 180°C/350°F/Gas Mark 4, for about 40-45 minutes, or until the meat is tender.

TIME: Preparation takes about 30 minutes, and cooking takes about 1 hour.

SERVING IDEA: Serve with creamed potatoes and green vegetables.

ROGNONS À LA DIJONNAISE

*Veal kidneys are lighter in colour and milder in flavour
than lamb's kidneys. Since they must be quickly cooked,
kidneys make an ideal sauté dish.*

SERVES 6

60g/2oz unsalted butter
3-4 whole veal kidneys
1-2 shallots, finely chopped
280ml/½ pint dry white wine
90g/3oz butter, softened
45ml/3 tbsps Dijon mustard
Salt, pepper and lemon juice to taste
30ml/2 tbsps chopped parsley

1. Melt the unsalted butter in a large sauté pan. Cut the kidneys into 2.5cm/1 inch pieces and remove any fat or core. When the butter stops foaming, add the kidneys and sauté them, uncovered, until they are light brown on all sides, about 10 minutes. Remove the kidneys from the pan and keep them warm.

2. Add the shallots to the pan and cook for about 1 minute, stirring frequently. Add the wine and bring to the boil, stirring constantly and scraping the pan to remove any browned juices. Allow to boil rapidly for 3-4 minutes until the wine is reduced to about 45ml/3 tbsps. Remove the pan from the heat.

3. Mix the remaining butter with the mustard, add salt and pepper and whisk the mixture into the reduced sauce. Return the kidneys to pan, add the lemon juice and parsley and cook over low heat for 1-2 minutes to heat through. Serve immediately.

TIME: Preparation takes about 25 minutes and cooking takes 15-17 minutes.

VARIATIONS: If veal kidneys are not available, use lamb kidneys instead.

TOSTADAS

*These are popular all over Mexico and the
toppings reflect the food available in each area.
They are delicious, but difficult to eat!*

MAKES 12

2 tsps oil
450g/1lb minced beef or pork
2 tsps chilli powder
1 tsp ground cumin
1 tsp ground coriander
1 tin refried beans
1 package tostada shells

Toppings
Shredded lettuce
Grated Cheddar cheese
Tomatoes, seeded and chopped
Sour cream
Olives
Prawns
Spring onions, chopped
Taco sauce

1. Cook the meat in the oil in a medium frying pan. Sprinkle on the spices and cook quickly to brown.

2. Reheat the beans and place the tostada shells on a baking sheet. Heat 2-3 minutes in a moderate oven.

3. Spread 15-30ml/1-2 tbsps of the beans on each tostada shells.

4. Top each shell with some of the beef mixture.

5. Add the topping ingredients in different combinations and serve immediately.

TIME: Preparation takes about 40 minutes and cooking takes about 10-15 minutes.

VARIATION: Add chopped green or red peppers to the list of toppings along with chopped green chillies or Jalapeño peppers and guacamole.

LEG OF LAMB WITH CHILLI SAUCE

*Give Sunday roast lamb a completely different
taste with a spicy orange sauce.*

SERVES 4

1kg/2¼ lb leg of lamb

Marinade
5ml/1 tsp cocoa powder
1.25ml/½ tsp cayenne pepper
2.5ml/½ tsp ground cumin
2.5cm/½ tsp paprika
2.5cm/½ tsp ground oregano
140ml/¼ pint water
140ml/¼ pint orange juice
140ml/¼ pint red wine
1 clove of garlic, crushed
30g/2 tbsps brown sugar
15ml/1 tbsp cornflour
Pinch salt
Orange slices and coriander to garnish

---

1. If the lamb has a lot of surface fat, trim slightly with a sharp knife. If possible, remove the paper-thin skin on the outside of the lamb. Place lamb in a shallow dish.

2. Mix together the marinade ingredients, except cornflour, and pour over the lamb, turning it well to coat completely. Cover and refrigerate for 12-24 hours, turning occasionally.

3. Drain the lamb, reserving the marinade, and place in a roasting pan. Cook in a preheated 180°C/350°F/Gas Mark 4 oven for about 2 hours until meat is cooked according to taste.

4. Baste occasionally with the marinade and pan juices.

5. Remove lamb to a serving dish and keep warm. Skim the fat from the top of the roasting pan with a large spoon and discard.

6. Pour remaining marinade into the pan juices in the roasting pan and bring to the boil, stirring to loosen the sediment. Mix cornflour with a small amount of water and add some of the liquid from the roasting pan. Gradually stir cornflour mixture into the pan and bring back to the boil.

7. Cook, stirring constantly, until thickened and clear. Add more orange juice, wine or water as necessary.

8. Garnish the lamb with orange slices and sprigs of coriander. Pour over some of the sauce and serve the rest separately.

TIME: Preparation takes about 15 minutes, with 12-14 hours for the lamb to marinate. Cooking takes about 2 hours for the lamb and 20 minutes to finish the sauce.

SERVING IDEA: Serve with rice or boiled potatoes and vegetables.

LAMB KORMA

*One of the best known Indian curries, a korma is
rich, spicy and a traditional favourite.*

SERVES 4

3 tbsps vegetable oil
1 medium onion, sliced
2.5cm/1 inch piece cinnamon stick
6 cloves
Seeds of 6 small cardamoms
1 bay leaf
1 tsp black cumin seeds
2 tsps ginger paste, or grated fresh ginger
1 tsp garlic paste, or 2 cloves garlic,
    crushed
450g/1lb shoulder of lamb, cubed
1 tsp chilli powder
1 tsp ground coriander
2 tsps ground cumin
½ tsp ground turmeric
140ml/¼ pint natural yogurt
160ml/6fl oz water
Salt to taste
1 tbsp ground almonds
2 green chillies, halved and seeded
2 sprigs fresh coriander leaves, chopped

1. Fry the onion in the oil until golden
brown. Add the cinnamon, cloves,
cardamoms, bay leaf and the cumin seeds.
Fry for 1 minute.

2. Add the ginger and garlic pastes and
the cubed lamb. Sprinkle over the chilli
powder, ground coriander, cumin and
turmeric and mix together well.

3. Stir in the yogurt, cover the pan and
cook over a moderate heat for 10-15
minutes, stirring occasionally.

4. Add the water and salt to taste, re-cover
and simmer gently for 30-40 minutes, or
until the meat is tender.

5. Just before serving, add the almonds,
chillies and coriander leaves. Stir in a little
more water if necessary, to produce a
medium-thick gravy.

TIME: Preparation takes about 15 minutes, and cooking takes about 40-50 minutes.

SERVING IDEA: Serve with boiled rice, or chapattis.

SZECHUAN MEATBALLS

*Szechuan is a region of China that lends its name to a style of
cooking which includes many spices, most notably ginger.
The spicy nature of these dishes means they require no salt.*

SERVES 4

90g/3oz blanched almonds
450g/1lb minced beef
5ml/1 tsp grated fresh ginger
1 clove garlic, crushed
½ large green pepper, seeded and chopped
Dash of Szechuan, chilli, or Tabasco sauce
30ml/2 tbsps soy sauce
45ml/3 tbsps soy sauce
120ml/4 fl oz vegetable stock
15ml/1 tbsp rice wine or white wine
  vinegar
10ml/2 tsps honey
15ml/1 tbsp sherry
15ml/1 tbsp cornflour
4 spring onions, chopped

1. Spread the almonds evenly onto a grill pan, and grill under a low heat for 3-4 minutes, or until lightly toasted. Stir the almonds often to prevent them from burning.

2. Chop the almonds coarsely using a large sharp knife.

3. In a large bowl, combine the chopped almonds with the meat, ginger, garlic, green pepper, Szechuan sauce, and the 2 tbsps of soy sauce. Use a wooden spoon, or your hands, to ensure that the ingredients are well blended.

4. Divide the mixture into 16 and roll each piece into small meatballs on a lightly floured board.

5. Heat a little oil in a large frying pan and lay in about half of the meatballs in a single layer.

6. Cook the meatballs over a low heat for about 20 minutes, turning them frequently until they are well browned all over.

7. Transfer to a serving dish and keep warm while you cook the remaining meatballs. Set aside as before.

8. Stir the 3 tbsps soy sauce, stock and vinegar into the frying pan and bring to the boil. Boil briskly for about 30 seconds.

9. Add the honey and stir until dissolved.

10. Blend the sherry and cornflour together in a small bowl, and add this into the hot sauce. Cook, stirring all the time, until thickened.

11. Arrange the meatballs on a serving dish and sprinkle with the sliced spring onions. Pour the sauce over, and serve.

TIME: Preparation takes about 20 minutes and cooking takes 40 minutes.

SERVING IDEA: Serve with boiled rice and a tomato salad.

COUNTRY CAPTAIN CHICKEN

*A flavourful dish named for a sea captain with
a taste for the spicy cuisine of India.*

SERVES 6

1.5kg/3lbs chicken portions
Seasoned flour
90ml/6 tbsps oil
1 medium onion, chopped
1 medium green pepper, seeded and
  chopped
1 clove garlic, crushed
Pinch salt and pepper
10ml/2 tsps curry powder
2 x 400g/14oz cans tomatoes
10ml/2 tsps chopped parsley
5ml/1 tsp chopped marjoram
60ml/4 tbsps currants or raisins
120g/4oz blanched almond halves

1. Remove skin from the chicken and
dredge with flour, shaking off the excess.

2. Heat the oil and brown the chicken on
all sides until golden. Remove to an
ovenproof casserole.

3. Pour off all but 30ml/2 tbsps of the oil.
Add the onion, pepper and garlic and
cook slowly to soften.

4. Add the seasonings and curry powder
and cook, stirring frequently, for 2
minutes. Add the tomatoes, parsley, and
marjoram and bring to the boil. Pour the
sauce over the chicken, cover and cook in
a preheated 180°C/350°F/Gas Mark 4 oven
for 45 minutes. Add the currants or raisins
during the last 15 minutes.

5. Meanwhile, toast the almonds in the
oven on a baking sheet along with the
chicken. Stir them frequently and watch
carefully. Sprinkle over the chicken just
before serving.

TIME: Preparation takes about 30 minutes and cooking takes about 50 minutes.

SERVING IDEA: If desired, serve the chicken with an accompaniment of rice.

FIVE-SPICED PORK

*Five spice is a ready-prepared spicy powder which can easily
be obtained from delicatessens or supermarkets.*

SERVES 4

450g/1lb fillet pork
60ml/4 tbsps sesame oil
One 2.5cm/1 inch piece fresh ginger,
  peeled and chopped
1 tsp black peppercorns
1 tsp five spice powder
5 tbsps dry sherry
140ml/¼ pint light stock
2 tbsps honey
4 spring onions, cut into diagonal slices
60g/2oz bamboo shoots, shredded
1 ripe mango, peeled and flesh sliced

---

1. Using a sharp knife, finely slice the
pork fillets into thin strips.

2. Put the oil into a wok or large frying
pan, and heat gently. Add the ginger and
stir this into the oil. Fry quickly for 20-30
seconds.

3. Add the sliced meat to the wok and stir-
fry for 4-5 minutes, or until the meat is
well cooked and tender.

4. Stir the peppercorns, five spice powder,
sherry, stock and honey into the meat.
Mix well and bring to the boil.

5. Add all the remaining ingredients to the
wok and cook quickly, stirring all the time
for a further 3 minutes.

6. Serve immediately.

TIME: Preparation takes 25 minutes and cooking takes about 10 minutes.

VARIATION: Use chicken instead of pork in this recipe.

BEEF AND LEEK SKEWERS

*An unusual combination, these kebabs are
nutritious, as well as being very tasty.*

SERVES 4

4 tbsps caster sugar
2 tbsps tamarind extract
1 tbsp grated fresh ginger
140ml/¼ pint light soy sauce
Black pepper
450g/1lb rump steak
4 leeks
3 tbsps vegetable oil

1. In a large bowl, mix together the sugar, tamarind extract, ginger, soy sauce and pepper.

2. Cut the steak into 2.5cm/1 inch cubes. Trim the leeks to leave only the white and pale green parts and cut these into 2.5cm/1 inch pieces.

3. Put the beef and leeks into the marinade mixture and mix together thoroughly to coat evenly. Allow to stand for 30 minutes.

4. Thread the beef and leeks alternately onto thin wooden kebab skewers.

5. Heat the oil in a large shallow frying pan. Cook the kebabs in the oil, turning frequently to prevent them burning.

6. Add the marinade mixture to the pan and cook quickly, until it has reduced to a thick syrup.

7. Coat the kebabs with the marinade syrup before serving.

TIME: Preparation takes about 15 minutes, plus standing time of 30 minutes.
Cooking takes about 10 minutes.

SERVING IDEA: Serve with boiled rice and a mixed salad.

VEGETARIAN KEDGEREE

*A rich combination of spices makes this dish
extremely appetizing and colourful.*

SERVES 4-6

225g/8oz long grain rice
225g/8oz red lentils
750ml/1¼ pints tepid water
120g/4oz butter, or 4 tbsps vegetable oil
1 medium onion, chopped
½ tsp grated fresh root ginger
½ tsp finely chopped garlic
2.5cm/1 inch piece cinnamon stick
6 cloves
1 bay leaf
1 tsp ground coriander
¼ tsp ground turmeric
¼ tsp salt
2 green chillies, sliced in half lengthways
4-6 eggs

1. Wash the rice and lentils in 4-5 changes of cold water. Soak them in the tepid water for 30 minutes.

2. Heat the butter or oil in a large saucepan. Add the onion and fry for 2-3 minutes.

3. Add the ginger, garlic, cinnamon, cloves and bay leaf and fry for a further minute.

4. Drain the rice and lentils, reserving the water. Add the rice and lentils to the fried onions, together with the coriander, turmeric, salt and chillies.

5. Fry, stirring constantly, for 2-3 minutes, until the rice is thoroughly coated with the oil.

6. Pour over the reserved water and stir well. Bring the liquid to the boil, then stir once and cover the pan with a tight-fitting lid.

7. Reduce the heat and simmer for 8-10 minutes, without stirring, until the water has been absorbed and the rice and lentils are tender.

8. Meanwhile, boil the eggs. Serve the kedgeree topped with the hard-boiled eggs.

TIME: Preparation takes about 15 minutes, and cooking takes about 30 minutes.

BLACK-EYED BEAN CURRY

*Beans are excellent in curries as they
are healthy and absorb flavours well.*

SERVES 4

8oz black-eyed beans, washed and soaked
   overnight in water
1 onion, peeled and chopped
3 tbsps ghee or 3 tbsps salad or olive oil
1 bay leaf
1 inch cinnamon stick
1 tsp ginger paste
1 tsp garlic paste
¼ tsp ground turmeric
1 tsp ground coriander
1 tsp chilli powder
4 tomatoes, chopped
Salt to taste
2 green chillies, halved and chopped
2 sprigs fresh green coriander leaves,
   chopped

1. Boil drained beans in 2½ cups of water
for 20 minutes and allow to cool.

2. Fry onion in ghee or oil for 3-4
minutes. Add bay leaf, cinnamon, ginger
and garlic pastes and fry for 2 minutes.

3. Add turmeric, ground coriander, chilli
powder and stir the mixture well.

4. Add drained, boiled beans and
tomatoes. Add salt, chopped chilli and
fresh coriander leaves.

5. Cover and cook for 10-15 minutes on
gentle heat. The gravy should be thick.
Serve with rice.

TIME: Preparation takes 10 minutes and overnight soaking for the black-eyed beans.
Cooking takes 30-40 minutes.

MEXICAN PORK CASSEROLE

All the favourite flavours of Mexican cooking – chickpeas, beans, pepper,
chillies and spices – combine with pork in one easy-to-cook casserole.

SERVES 4

2 tsps oil
450g/1lb pork fillet, cut into 2.5cm/1 inch
   cubes
¼ tsp ground cumin
¼ tsp ground coriander
1 small onion, chopped
1 clove garlic, crushed
30g/1oz flour
15g/1 tbsp instant coffee
430ml/¾ pint stock
½ red pepper, diced
½ green pepper, diced
1 small chilli pepper, seeded and chopped
430g/15oz tinned red kidney beans, rinsed
430g/15oz tinned chickpeas, rinsed
Tortilla chips to garnish

1. Melt the oil in a frying pan and add the
pork. Fry for 5 minutes until the meat is
slightly browned.

2. Add the cumin, coriander, garlic, onion
and flour, and fry for 3-4 minutes. Transfer
the mixture to a casserole dish.

3. Dissolve the instant coffee in the stock
and add to the casserole, stirring well.

4. Add the peppers, cover, and cook in a
preheated oven at 180°C/350°F/Gas Mark
4 for 40 minutes, by which time the pork
should be tender.

5. Add the beans and chickpeas and
return to the oven for a further 4 minutes.
Serve with tortilla chips.

TIME: Preparation takes 15 minutes and cooking takes about 38 minutes.

VARIATION: Rice may be served instead of the tortilla chips as an accompaniment.

CHICKEN TANDOORI

*Although the true taste of tandoori (clay oven)
is not achieved, a very good result is obtained
by baking in a conventional oven.*

SERVES 4-6

1.5kg/3lb chicken, cut into 8-10 pieces
1 tsp garlic paste
1 tsp ginger paste
1 tsp ground black pepper
1 tsp paprika
¼ tsp red food colouring
1 tsp salt
3 tbsps brown vinegar
Juice of 1 lemon
180ml/6fl oz natural yogurt
1 tsp dry mint powder
Salad or olive oil
1 lemon, cut into wedges

1. Mix all the ingredients together, apart from the lemon wedges and oil.

2. Marinate chicken overnight.

3. Arrange chicken pieces on baking tray. Brush with oil and bake in a preheated oven at 190°C/375°F/Gas Mark 5, for 40 minutes, turning them over so that they bake evenly.

4. Bake until dry and well browned. Serve with lemon wedges.

TIME: Preparation takes 10 minutes, plus overnight marinating. Cooking takes 30-40 minutes.

SPICY RICE AND BEAN PILAFF

*A lively side dish or vegetarian main course, this recipe readily
takes to creative variations and even makes a good cold salad.*

SERVES 6-8

60ml/4 tbsps oil
225g/8oz long grain rice
1 onion, finely chopped
1 green pepper, seeded and chopped
1 tsp each ground cumin and
    coriander
Dash Tabasco sauce
Salt
1 ltr/1¾ pints vegetable stock
450g/1lb tinned red kidney beans,
    drained and rinsed
450g/1lb tinned tomatoes, drained and
    coarsely chopped
Chopped parsley

1. Heat the oil in a casserole or a large,
deep saucepan.

2. Add the rice and cook until just turning
opaque. Add the onion, pepper and
cumin and coriander. Cook gently for a
further 2 minutes.

3. Add the Tabasco, salt, stock and beans
and bring to the boil. Cover and cook
about 45 minutes, or until the rice is
tender and most of the liquid is absorbed.

4. Remove from the heat and add the
tomatoes, stirring them in gently. Leave to
stand, covered, for 5 minutes.

5. Fluff up the mixture with a fork and
sprinkle with parsley to serve.

TIME: Preparation takes about 25 minutes and cooking takes about 50 minutes.

SERVING IDEA: Serve with bread and a salad for a light vegetarian meal.
Serve as a side dish with meat or poultry, or cheese and egg dishes.

VARIATION: The recipe may be made with 450g/1lb fresh tomatoes, peeled,
seeded and coarsely chopped.

CURRIED PORK STEW

*This savoury stew requires long,
slow cooking to bring out its flavour.*

SERVES 4

900g/2lb pork shoulder, cut in 5cm/2 inch
   cubes
Oil
2 medium onions, cut in 5cm/2 inch pieces
1 large green pepper, seeded and cut in
   5cm/2 inch pieces
15ml/1 tbsp curry powder
2 cloves garlic, crushed
450g/1lb canned tomatoes
45ml/3 tbsps tomato purée
140ml/¼ pint water or beef stock
30ml/2 tbsps cider vinegar
1 bay leaf
2.5ml/½ tsp dried mint
Salt and a few drops Tabasco sauce

1. Heat about 30ml/2 tbsps oil in a large
sauté or frying pan. When hot, add the
pork cubes in two batches. Brown over
high heat for about 5 minutes per batch.

2. Remove to a plate. Add more oil if
necessary and cook the onions and
pepper to soften slightly. Add the curry
powder and garlic and cook for 1 minute
more.

3. Add the tomatoes, their juice and the
tomato purée. Stir in the water or stock
and vinegar breaking up the tomatoes
slightly. Add bay leaf, mint and salt.

4. Transfer to a flameproof casserole dish.
Bring the mixture to the boil and then
cook slowly for about 1½ hours, covered.

5. When the meat is completely tender,
skim any fat from the surface of the sauce,
remove the bay leaf and add a few drops
of Tabasco sauce to taste.

TIME: Preparation takes about 25 minutes and cooking takes about 1½ hours.

SERVING IDEA: Serve with a spicy pilaff and Nann bread which is
available from Indian grocers.

CHILLI ROJA

*Beef, red onions, red pepper, paprika, tomatoes
and red beans all go into this zesty stew.*

SERVES 6-8

900g/2lbs beef chuck, cut into 2.5cm/
   1 inch pieces
Oil
1 large red onion, coarsely chopped
2 cloves garlic, crushed
2 red pepper, seeded and cut into 2.5cm/
   1 inch pieces
1-2 red chillies, seeded and finely chopped
45ml/3 tbsps mild chilli powder
1 tbsp cumin
1 tbsp paprika
850ml/1½ pints beer, water or stock
225g/8oz tinned tomatoes, puréed
30ml/2 tbsps tomato purée
225g/8oz tinned red kidney beans, drained
Pinch of salt
6 ripe tomatoes, peeled, seeded and diced

1. Pour about 60ml/4 tbsps oil into a large saucepan or flameproof casserole. When hot, brown the meat in small batches over moderately high heat for about 5 minutes per batch.

2. Set aside the meat on a plate or in the lid of the casserole. Lower the heat and cook the onion, garlic, red peppers and chillies for about 5 minutes. Add the chilli powder, cumin and paprika and cook for 1 minute further. Pour on the liquid and add the tinned tomatoes, tomato purée and the meat.

3. Cook slowly for about 1½ -2 hours. Add the beans about 45 minutes before the end of cooking time.

4. When the meat is completely tender, add salt to taste and serve garnished with the diced tomatoes.

TIME: Preparation takes about 25 minutes and cooking takes about 1½ -2 hours.

VARIATION: The chilli may be made with pork shoulder, with a mixture of beef and pork or minced beef or pork.

TOMATO BEEF STIR-FRY

*East meets West in a dish that is lightning-fast to
cook and tastes like a "barbeque" sauced stir-fry.*

SERVES 4

450g/1lb sirloin or rump steak
2 cloves garlic, crushed
90ml/6 tbsps wine vinegar
90ml/6 tbsps oil
Pinch sugar, salt and pepper
1 bay leaf
15ml/1 tbsp ground cumin
1 small red pepper, seeded and sliced
1 small green pepper, seeded and sliced
60g/2oz baby sweetcorn
4 spring onions, shredded
Oil for frying

Tomato Sauce
8 fresh ripe tomatoes, peeled, seeded
  and chopped
60ml/4 tbsps oil
1 medium onion, finely chopped
1-2 green chillies, finely chopped
1-2 cloves garlic, crushed
6 sprigs fresh coriander
45ml/3 tbsps tomato purée

1. Slice the meat thinly across the grain.
Combine in a plastic bag with the next 6
ingredients. Tie the bag and toss the
ingredients inside to coat. Place in a bowl
and leave for about 4 hours.

2. Heat the oil for the sauce and cook the
onion, chillies and garlic to soften but not
brown. Add remaining sauce ingredients
and cook for about 15 minutes over gentle
heat. Purée in a food processor until
smooth.

3. Heat a frying pan and add the meat in
three batches, discarding the marinade.
Cook to brown and set aside. Add about
30ml/2 tbsps of oil and cook the peppers
for about 2 minutes. Add the corn and
onions and return the meat to the pan.
Cook for a further 1 minute and add the
sauce. Cook to heat through and serve
immediately.

TIME: Preparation takes about 25 minutes, with 4 hours for marinating the meat.
The sauce takes about 15 minutes to cook and the remaining ingredients
need about 6-7 minutes.

ROGAN JOSH

*A classic curry which is subtle
enough to suit all tastes.*

SERVES 4

---

1 onion, peeled and sliced
2½ tbsps ghee or 4 tbsps salad or olive oil
6 green cardamoms
4 large cardamoms
6 cloves
2 bay leaves
2.5cm/1 inch cinnamon stick
2.5cm/1 inch root ginger, crushed
3 cloves garlic, crushed
1lb boned lean lamb or beef, cut into cubes
1 tsp ground cumin
1 tsp chilli powder
2 tsps paprika
1 tsp ground coriander
180ml/6fl oz natural yogurt
1 tsp salt
2 tbsps chopped, blanched almonds
1 tbsp ground poppyseeds
380ml/13fl oz water
1 pinch saffron

---

1. Fry onion in ghee or oil until lightly browned.

2. Stir-fry cardamoms, cloves, bay leaves and cinnamon for 1 minute.

3. Add ginger and garlic paste, stir and add the meat. Sprinkle on, one at a time, the cumin, chilli, paprika and coriander. Fry the mixture for 2 minutes.

4. Add yogurt and salt; cover and cook for 5-7 minutes until dry, and oil separates.

5. Add almonds and poppyseeds. Stir-fry for 1-2 minutes and add water. Cover and cook for 40-50 minutes, simmering gently until meat is tender and the mixture is fairly dry. Sprinkle with saffron.

6. Cover and cook gently for another 5-10 minutes, taking care not to burn the meat. Stir the mixture a few times to mix saffron. Rogan josh is a dry dish, with moist spices around the meat.

TIME: Preparation takes 20 minutes and cooking takes 1 hour.

SPICED CRÈME BRÛLÉE

A delicious variation on a classic dessert.

SERVES 4

280ml/½ pint milk
280ml/½ pint double cream
1 stick of cinnamon
2 tsps coriander seeds, lightly crushed
1 vanilla pod
4 egg yolks
½ tsp cornflour
90g/3oz caster sugar
Demerara, or soft light brown sugar

1. Pour the milk and cream into a heavy-based saucepan. Add the spices and vanilla pod and heat gently until almost, but not quite, boiling. Allow to cool slightly.

2. Beat the egg yolks, cornflour and sugar together until light in colour.

3. Strain the milk and cream mixture gradually onto the egg yolks, beating between additions.

4. Pour the egg and cream mixture back into the pan and place over a gentle heat. Bring the mixture to just below boiling point very slowly, stirring constantly, to prevent curdling. Continue stirring, until the mixture has thickened enough to coat the back of a spoon.

5. Remove the custard from the heat and strain it into four ramekins or custard cups. Chill until set.

6. When set, put the custards into a roasting pan and surround them with ice. Preheat a grill to the highest temperature.

7. Sprinkle a thin layer of sugar over the top of each custard and place under a grill, until the sugar melts and caramelizes.

8. Before serving, chill the custards in the refrigerator, until the sugar layer is crisp.

TIME: Preparation takes about 15 minutes, and cooking takes 20-30 minutes.

COOK'S TIP: If the egg mixture curdles, stand the saucepan in a bowl of cold water and whisk it rapidly with a balloon or electric whisk.

SERVING IDEA: Serve with crisp biscuits and/or fresh fruit.

APPLE NUT TART

*The sweet, spicy flavour of cinnamon blends perfectly
with the apples and nuts in this traditional dessert.*

SERVES 6

250g/9oz plain flour
150g/5oz caster sugar
135g/4½ oz butter, cut into pieces
1 egg
450g/1lb dessert apples, peeled, cored
 and sliced
60g/2oz hazelnuts, coarsely ground
1 tsp ground cinnamon
Juice of 1 lemon
3 tbsps apricot brandy (optional)
120g/4oz apricot jam
60g/2oz chopped hazelnuts

1. Sieve together the flour and 120g/4oz
of the sugar into a bowl. Rub in the
butter, until the mixture resembles fine
breadcrumbs.

2. Make a well in the centre of the flour
mixture, add the egg and mix using a
knife or, as the mixture becomes firmer,
your fingers. Continue kneading the until
it forms a smooth dough.

3. Wrap the dough in greaseproof paper
and chill for at least 30 minutes in the
refrigerator.

4. Roll out the pastry and use it to line a
20cm/8 inch greased pie dish.

5. Layer the apple slices and the ground
hazelnuts in the pastry case. Sprinkle over
the cinnamon, remaining sugar, lemon
juice and apricot brandy if using.

6. Put the apricot jam into a small
saucepan and heat through gently until it
has melted. Pour the melted jam over the
layers of apple and hazelnut.

7. Sprinkle with the chopped hazelnuts
and bake in a preheated oven, 220°C/
425°F/Gas Mark 7, for 35-40 minutes, or
until the fruit is soft and the tart is golden
brown.

TIME: Preparation takes about 20 minutes, and cooking takes about 40 minutes.

SERVING IDEA: Serve with clotted cream.

Spiced Fruit Salad

Sweet and spicy, this fruit salad is certainly out of the ordinary.

SERVES 6

1 mango, peeled and cubed
1 small pineapple, skinned, cored and
  cubed
2 bananas, peeled and sliced
12 lychees, peeled and stones removed
2 kiwi fruit, peeled and sliced
1 small melon, peeled and cubed
2 oranges, peeled and segmented
120g/4oz palm sugar, or light brown sugar
1 tsp tamarind extract
2 tbsps water
Juice of 1 lime
2.5cm/1 inch piece fresh ginger, grated
½ tsp ground nutmeg
½ tsp ground cinnamon
½ tsp ground coriander

1. Prepare all the fruit over a bowl, to catch the juice. Arrange the prepared fruit in a serving bowl.

2. In a small bowl, combine the sugar with the tamarind, water, lime juice and spices. Stir this into the prepared fruit, together with any fruit juice, mixing well to blend thoroughly.

3. Chill the fruit salad for at least 1 hour before serving, stirring it again before you do.

TIME: Preparation takes about 30 minutes, plus chilling time of at least 1 hour.

COOK'S TIP: If tamarind extract is unobtainable, substitute the juice of half a lemon and omit the water as well.

RHUBARB TART

An ideal dessert to make when rhubarb is plentiful.
The juice which is left over makes a refreshing
drink when diluted with chilled soda water.

SERVES 6

900g/2lbs rhubarb, cut into 2.5cm/1 inch
   pieces
525g/1lb 3oz caster sugar
120g/4oz butter
3 eggs
2 tbsps white wine
250g/9oz plain flour
2 tsps baking powder
140ml/¼ pint soured cream
1 tsp ground cinnamon
60g/2oz ground almonds
Icing sugar, to dredge

---

1. Put the rhubarb into a bowl and sprinkle with 400g/14oz of the sugar. Cover and allow to stand for 1-2 hours.

2. Cream the butter with 90g/3oz of the remaining sugar, until it is light and fluffy.

3. Beat one of the eggs and add this and the wine to the creamed butter and sugar. Sift in the flour and baking powder and mix together well.

4. Knead the base mixture together until it forms a smooth dough. Wrap the dough in greaseproof paper and chill for 30 minutes in the refrigerator.

5. Roll out the dough on a lightly floured board and use it to line a well-greased, loose-based, or spring-clip, 25cm/10 inch round flan tin, pressing the pastry well into the base and up the sides of the tin.

6. Strain the rhubarb and arrange the pieces in the pastry case. Bake in a preheated oven, 180°C/350°F/Gas Mark 4, for 30 minutes.

7. Beat together the cream and the remaining eggs and sugar. Stir in the cinnamon and ground almonds, mixing well to ensure they are thoroughly blended.

8. Remove the flan from the oven and pour the cream topping over the rhubarb. Return the flan to the oven and cook at the same temperature for a further 20-25 minutes, or until the topping is golden brown.

9. Ease the flan out of the tin and cool completely before dredging with icing sugar and serving.

TIME: Preparation takes about 30 minutes, plus 1-2 hours standing time for the rhubarb. Cooking takes 30 minutes for the base, followed by 20-25 minutes for the topping.

VARIATION: Use 900g/2lbs stoned and quartered red plums instead of the rhubarb.

SPICED BISCUITS

Crunchy and wholesome, these spicy biscuits are a tea-time treat.

MAKES ABOUT 15 BISCUITS

120g/4oz wholewheat flour
½ tsp bicarbonate of soda
1 tsp ground cinnamon
1 tsp ground mixed spice
60g/2oz rolled oats
90g/3oz soft brown sugar
90g/3oz butter
1 tbsp golden syrup
1 tbsp milk

1. Put the flour, bicarbonate of soda, cinnamon, mixed spice, oats and sugar into a bowl and stir well to blend thoroughly. Make a well in the centre.

2. In a small saucepan, melt the butter with the syrup and milk over a gentle heat.

3. Pour the melted mixture into the dry ingredients and beat well, until the mixture forms a smooth, pliable dough.

4. Divide the mixture into about 15 small balls. Place these onto lightly greased baking sheets, with a wet spoon, and bake in a preheated oven, 180°C/350°F/Gas Mark 4, for about 15 minutes, or until golden brown.

5. Allow the biscuits to cool on the baking sheet before removing them.

TIME: Preparation takes about 20 minutes and cooking takes about 15 minutes.

VARIATION: Substitute ground ginger for the cinnamon and mixed spice.

Index